Be A Lion At Heart

This book is dedicated to anyone who has ever been bullied

or who has ever bullied anyone.

This story is based off of true events.

Names have been changed.

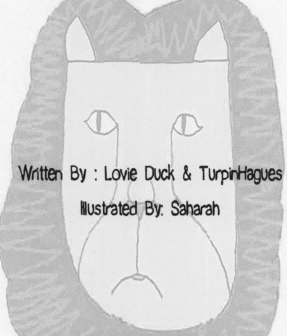

Written By : Lovie Duck & TurpinHagues

Illustrated By: Saharah

Library of Congress Control Number: 2017903830
CreateSpace Independent Publishing Platform, North Charleston, SC:

My name is Timothy. When I was 8 years old, I would try to climb up walls. I loved to jump on all kinds of furniture in my house too. My mom would say "Get down, Timothy, your acting like an animal!"

My dream to be a super hero,
and the best climber in the world
came to a sudden end.

Meen was never a part of my life before. I hadn't met him until one day I was playing at the park. He came up to me, and pushed me down onto the ground for no reason at all!

Meen pushed me down as hard as he could! I tried to be brave, but I felt very sad inside as the other kids laughed at me.
No one tried to help me.

Meen made me feel ashamed and embarrassed.
I was so embarrassed that I
decided not to tell anyone that he was bullying me.

None of the other kids told on him either

I thought that maybe he wouldn't bother me anymore
if I didn't tell anyone how he was treating me.
I was wrong, he bullied me even more than before!

One day my friend, sister, and I decided to go to the park. Meen was there. This time I tried to stay far away from him. That didn't work because without notice he ran up behind me, tackled me to the ground, and kicked me in the head.

With a brave lion heart,
my baby sister ran to find help for me. I was hurt very badly,
and my sister was hurt to see what Meen had done to me.

Meen severely fractured my hip. I had to have emergency surgery, and the doctor put a big screw in my hip

to keep the bones together.

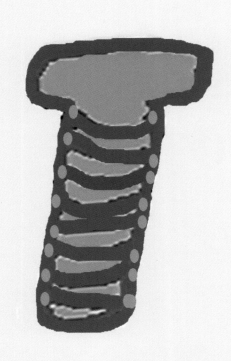

The blood supply in my hip was severely damaged.
In the long run,
I will have to get a total hip replacement because of it.

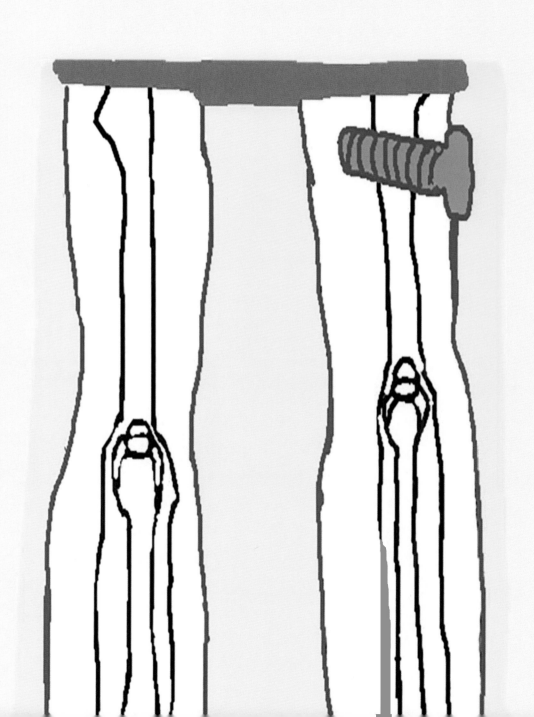

My mom is a lion at heart,
she told the police what Meen had done to me.

He got into big trouble.

It hurts me when I think back about how I was bullied,
but then I look at my life now, and how much stronger it has made me.

I believe that I have more than a brave heart.
I have learned to be a lion at heart for others, just like my sister was for me.

I feel happy knowing that I can help you by telling you to be positive, stay strong, and be a lion at heart!

If you're being bullied,
please don't bury it on the inside...tell someone!
Go to someone you can trust,
and seek help before it's too late.
Be a lion at heart!

If you are bullying someone,
please understand that you're not only effecting that person,
but you're effecting entire families.
Stop what you are doing,
and seek help from someone you can trust.
Be a lion at heart!

A Letter From The Author:

Thank you for reading my story. It has not been an easy journey, but I am stronger now! I have created a safe, social environment for you to enjoy. Please visit my new website that will launch in April 2017! You are invited!!

www.thesocialencouragementnetwork.com

Thank you for reading my story!

Sincerely,
Lovie Duck

15322448R00015

Printed in Great Britain
by Amazon